The MacLehose Trail

ISBN 962-201-886-6

First edition   1992
Second printing 1993
Third printing   1993
Fourth printing 1995
Second edition   1998

THE CHINESE UNIVERSITY PRESS
The Chinese University of Hong Kong
SHA TIN, N.T., HONG KONG.
Fax: +852 2603 6692
     +852 2603 7355
E-mail: cup@cuhk.edu.hk
Web-site: http://www.cuhk.edu.hk/cupress/wl.htm

Printed in Hong Kong

The MacLehose Trail

麥理浩徑

Produced by
Tim Nutt · Chris Bale · Tao Ho

Revised and Updated

The Chinese University Press

References

1. Pak Tam Chung
2. High Island Reservoir
3. Urn Island
4. Rocky Harbour
5. Bluff Island
6. Basalt Island
7. Pyramid Rock
8. Town Island
9. Hole Island
10. Long Ke
11. Sai Wan
12. Big Wave Bay
13. Ham Tin
14. Tai Long
15. Sharp Peak
16. Chek Keng
17. Long Harbour
18. Tap Mun
19. Pak Tam Au
20. Ngau Yee Shek Shan
21. Ngam Tau Shan
22. Cheung Sheung
23. Lui Ta Shek
24. Kai Kung Shan
25. Tolo Channel
26. Kei Ling Ha
27. Wong Chuk Yuen
28. Ma On Shan
29. The Hunch Backs
30. Pyramid Hill
31. Ngong Ping
32. Sai Kung
33. Port Shelter
34. Silverstrand
35. Buffalo Hill
36. Heather Pass
37. Gilwell Scout Campsite
38. Tate's Cairn
39. Tate's Ridge
40. Fei Ngo Shan
41. Unicorn Ridge
42. Lion Rock
43. Beacon Hill
44. Eagle's Nest
45. Tai Po Road
46. Kowloon Reservoirs
47. Smugglers' Ridge
48. Shing Mun Reservoir
49. Needle Hill
50. Sha Tin
51. Grassy Hill
52. Lead Mine Pass
53. Tai Po
54. Kwun Yam Shan
55. Tai Mo Shan
56. Shek Kong
57. Route Twisk
58. Chuen Lung
59. Tsuen Wan
60. Kwai Chung
61. Ngau Liu
62. Ho Pui Reservoir
63. Tin Fu Tsai
64. Tai Lam Chung Reservoir
65. So Kwun Wat
66. Lok On Pai Desalination Plant
67. Perowne Camp
68. Tuen Mun
69. Castle Peak
70. Deep Bay
71. Lantau
72. Victoria Harbour
73. Hong Kong Island
74. Kowloon
75. Kai Tak
76. Chai Wan

Walking the MacLehose Trail

The MacLehose Trail is for everyone to explore and enjoy. Walks can be short or long, easy or tough, and each season shows the Trail in a new light.

Maps

The route is generally well marked but a good map is essential. The Countryside Series is excellent and the three sheets which cover the Trail are Sai Kung and Clear Water Bay, Central New Territories and Northwest New Territories. A large scale black and white map of the whole Trail is also available. These maps cost $45–$50 each and are available from Government Publications Centre, Ground Floor, Low Block, Queensway Government Offices (2537 1910).

Background Information

The Country Parks Authority produces a good, clear, bilingual leaflet about the Trail, which contains useful tips and directions, grades each stage according to its difficulty and indicates how long the walker will take to complete it. For further information, contact the Country Parks Authority on 2420 0529 or visit its website at www.afdparks.gov.hk.

Oxfam Hong Kong's book, *Trailwalker*, celebrates the annual charity event organised along the Trail. Copies at $99 are available from Oxfam Hong Kong, 9/F Breakthrough Centre, 191 Woosung Street, Jordan, Kowloon (2520 2525).

Contents

Why a Trail, and anyway why MacLehose? Others did the work, we were merely enthusiastic. It was like this; when my wife and I first worked in Hong Kong in 1959, the high villages of the New Territories were still occupied and the fields tilled. The old stone paths of the Ching dynasty were still in use, if sometimes mended by the Kadoorie Agricultural Association and Government. The brush of loads on carrying poles kept the growth back from the paths. It must have been not unlike its original state. After a week in the city it was a life-saver, it was a different and beautiful world and we explored it and its flora every weekend we could.

When we returned to Hong Kong it had changed. The young people of the remote villages had left for the city, the houses were deserted and the fields unworked. Many of the paths were overgrown. But the magic of the mountains with their shrubs and flowers, and the contrast with the city, were still there and attracted us as much as ever. Room for open-air recreation in the city was woefully short, so the Government began to encourage more people to enjoy the countryside. But the question was: would there be a countryside to enjoy?

The Trail was born out of the Country Parks, and the Parks were to preserve the countryside.

Foreword

Without them Hong Kong would have had no lung, no undeveloped areas, so a line had to be drawn. Drawing it to take account of so many conflicting interests was a nightmare, but it was done by a combination of devoted people. Some names I have forgotten, but I do remember Denis Bray, David Akers-Jones, Martin Lewis, John Wholey and above all Ted Nichols, the Director of Agriculture and Fisheries. Between them they got the Parks marked out, the legislation through (Unofficials were most supportive) and the Country Parks division and its administration set up. Ted carried it forward with great energy and imagination.

He saw that if the public were to picnic and walk in the mountains with safety, they should be encouraged to use recognised sites and paths where help could be made available and litter and fire controlled. So his team built camp and picnic sites, and marked and mended the principal paths, and they eventually joined up village paths and grass cutters' tracks to make a continuous path through open countryside from Mirs Bay to the Pearl River, to publicise what a lot of walking room there was in unspoilt country, and so attract people to walk in it.

This was done; he then asked if it might be named after us. We had merely cheered on him and his team, nevertheless we were pleased and flattered; this was indeed something we would like to be associated with. So Ted's East/West path became The MacLehose Trail. Sadly the logo invented for it will immortalise MacLehose as the perpetrator of intense fatigue in exhausted bodies under heavy loads on semi-perpendicular slopes. What will be will be, but the Trail was a brilliant idea and I am delighted it has become so popular, so congratulations to Tim Nutt, Chris Bale, T. L. Tsim and Tao Ho for recording in their book the great variety the Trail has to offer. May it imbue others with their enthusiasm. ●

Lord MacLehose
August, 1992

"Dad, I am going to enter the Trailwalker with some friends from school next month." "Sounds fun, but what is it ?" "It's a trail up in the New Territories, starting in Sai Kung somewhere and finishing up in Tuen Mun—about 100 kilometres, I think. We were wondering whether you and Mum would support us, you know, be our backup."

Little did I know that this simple conversation would set in motion a chain of events that would occupy a very high percentage of my free time during the next three years.

The MacLehose Trail is a familiar name to many people and I am sure that most of us have enjoyed walking parts of the Trail during weekend visits to the country parks. In November each year the Trailwalker weekend gathers together a fascinating mix of people all eager to meet the challenge of completing this 100 kilometres trail within 48 hours in support of the Trailwalker Charitable Trust. My daughter managed to finish in 46 hours—as her backup, I remember sleeping briefly for an hour somewhere at Lead Mine Pass. I recall phantoms appearing from the mist up in the hills and the kindness shown by the Gurkhas as they dressed the blisters and bandaged the aching limbs. It was a very stimulating experience.

I have another daughter, just as determined, and the following year her team from school managed to break the family record by eight hours.

Introduction

Seeing these brave souls hobbling to victory amid warm cheers from the waiting Gurkhas I realized that very few of the walkers had any clear visual memory of the MacLehose Trail.

I was curious to find out the measure of the Trail and to confirm my belief that up in the hills, silhouettes reminiscent of Chinese paintings were there for the searching. Excited and not knowing what to expect, I began climbing the hill towards High Island Reservoir at the start of the MacLehose Trail. The morning light greeted me with a kindness, extending a warmth I have not known since I was a child. Looking across the reservoir towards Long Ke Wan, the light was playing on the water, reflecting the joyful sight of dawn. I was very moved and felt a sense of privilege at being allowed to enjoy this unique moment….This was the memory of a Chinese painting where the brush stroke is delivered in an instant of time, where perception and purpose climax in form and substance. My beliefs were so quickly confirmed and I was eager to continue to let the changing views and moods reveal themselves.

Since that first outing, I kept to my programme, walking each stage in sequence, usually early in the morning when the light is kind and not tired from a busy day. The scenes and surprises waiting for the traveller complement the romantic names handed down by history: Smugglers' Ridge, Buffalo Hill and the Hunch Backs. With real beaches, rolling hills, valleys, bamboo groves, cityscenes, harbours and forest tracks, this Trail must be a heritage that no other city can boast or rival.

Since those days, I have walked the various stages of the Trail many times, witnessing the seasons and the moods, every journey a new experience, every trek a new beginning. It is for me the most fascinating, the most uplifting and most satisfying walk anywhere in the world.

To share this with others, the idea of a book seemed a natural progression. Encouraged by friends, I managed to coerce Chris Bale, T. L. Tsim and Tao Ho to join me in committing time and our own individual talents freely, with the understanding that any profits from the book would be donated to the Trailwalker Charitable Trust.

I hope good memories come to mind for the old hands and that new readers are encouraged to follow the Trail and experience as we have a part of Hong Kong that really does exist and is there to be enjoyed and explored.🜚

Tim Nutt
August, 1992

Pak Tam Chung

Urn Island

High Island
Reservoir

Long Ke

Rocky Harbour

from Pak Tam Chung
to Long Ke
10.6km
北潭涌至浪茄

Awhite egret flies low over the stony river bed, where water trickles and chortles on its way to the sea. Above the hiss of cicadas pipes the crazy, spiralling song of the koel, and the first weak rays of sunshine pierce the early morning haze. The walker sets off on Stage One of the MacLehose Trail.

The still waters of High Island Reservoir are grey green in the pale morning light, barely reflecting the dark hills. The water level is low, and dead trees, long submerged, stand exposed at the shoreline, a thin, forlorn forest of grey stalks.

On the other side of the track is the High Island Detention Centre, the prison which for years was home to thousands of boat people from Vietnam. The people have gone but the prison is still there, its empty huts and abandoned sentry posts looking like a film set without its stars.

Brighter colours appear beside the track. Splash of White, with its bright white petals splayed out prissily like collars around yellow flowers, and Lantana, with its cheerful combinations of white and pink, red and orange, orange and purple, red and yellow.

The long walk beside the reservoir leads to a lookout point across Rocky Harbour, which is flecked with surf as the waves roll over the rocks. The harbour is dotted with islands—Town Island, Hole Island, Basalt, Bluff and Pyramid Rock. High Island was the biggest of all until it was linked to the mainland when the reservoir was built in the late Seventies. A double dam faces the sea, with 7,000 huge concrete knuckles scattered across the outer wall to break the force of the waves. One of the knuckles has been painted a lurid blue and placed on top of the dam, like a misplaced modern sculpture, a strange memorial to five men who died while working on the reservoir.

At last, the walker leaves the road and the reservoir, and strikes off over rougher ground. Butterflies crisscross the path—orange flecked with brown, vivid yellow, white with dainty gold spots, deep crimson. Ahead lies Long Ke, a beautiful beach of white sand, clear water and a perfect backdrop of green hills. On a summer's day, the pleasure boats sit offshore while children splash in the sea. In winter, the wind blows a stinging sandstorm across the beach. Whatever the season, Long Ke is the walker's first indication of the treasures which the Trail has to offer, corners of Hong Kong which city folk can scarcely believe.◐

A clear prospect stretching to the ends of the earth.

清 景 無 限

Urn Island

六頭洲

糧船灣海

Rocky Harbour

High Island Reservoir

萬宜水庫

浪茄*Long Ke*

Chek Keng

Pak Tam Au

Ham Tin

Big Wave Bay

Sai Wan

Long Ke

Stage 2

*from Long Ke
to Pak Tam Au
13.5km*
浪茄至北潭凹

The climb from Long Ke is steep and rough, but the reward is a view to lift the most jaded spirits—the blue green seas of Big Wave Bay, a line of four deserted beaches, old villages nestling into the hills, and Sharp Peak rising in the distance, a huge and ancient sentinel.

The mirrored towers of Central reflect one face of Hong Kong; she is smart, thoroughly modern and a shade pretentious. The markets of Mong Kok show her in a different light—loud, streetwise, tough. Here along her eastern coastline she reveals yet another side to her nature—mellow, timeless, true. The wind blows her hair and the green sea laps at her feet. This is Hong Kong— and she is beautiful.

The Trail leads over the hills to the first of the beaches, Sai Wan. Strong currents can make swimming dangerous, but on a hot day official warnings are no match for the temptation of clear water, sparkling in the afternoon sunshine, waves rushing to shore in a silver cascade.

A *kai do* chugs round from Sai Kung, delivering instant noodles, soft drinks and other supplies to a few small stores tucked away among the casuarina trees. In summer, the stores do brisk business. There are rooms to let and night-time parties on the beach. In winter, there are more dogs than people.

The path to the next beach at Ham Tin passes a solitary tomb, apparently the resting place of a man of some wealth and influence. His grave is overgrown, the stonework flaking and the blackened stubs of two incense sticks suggesting an ancestor forgotten. Forgotten, perhaps, but here a man would surely be at rest, gazing over the hills and soothed by the gentle rhythm of surf and wind.

At Ham Tin Wan, the Trail turns inland and the walker feels a sense of loss at leaving the coastline. The sound of the sea, the wind and the air of freedom have been an invigorating start to the Trail.

On a winter's day, there are few signs of life in Tai Long village, a few minutes walk up the valley. Most of the houses are bolted and barred. An old woman, bowed and unseeing, shuffles past a group of men playing cards, but there are no children. The ruins of a house which once commanded a grand view across the valley are now almost hidden in the undergrowth. The terraced fields, which stretch up the rocky slopes of Sharp Peak, are untended and overgrown.

Yet it is not difficult to picture Tai Long in years gone by as a thriving community. The fields would have been tended then, producing rice and vegetables. Cattle grazed the hills and fishing boats sailed from Ham Tin Wan. Today, on a summer weekend, a few villagers serve iced coffee and spaghetti to passing hikers. Recreation has replaced agriculture as the lifeblood of Tai Long.

After strolling since mid-morning—stopping for a swim at Long Ke, perhaps, or a plate of beef noodles in Sai Wan—the walker cuts through the hills above Chek Keng at sunset. The little bay is a pretty sight, with the path up to Pak Tam Au lit by street lamps that flicker in the gloaming like a distant row of candles.

In the winter hiking season there is a wonderful tranquility in Chek Keng. The lovely old houses are boarded up and the pathways are deserted. Two roly-poly black puppies play with a fishing net, the only signs of life. A Marine Police launch pulls away from the pier and heads out into Long Harbour, its engines growling and a broad white wake flowing behind, but within five minutes it is lost to view and the stillness returns.

The walker stops for a last look back across Chek Keng Bay, and there in the distance is Sharp Peak, the mountain that has dominated this stage of the Trail. Silhouetted against the night sky, dark and commanding, it has watched the walker's every step. Years ago it watched people walk out of these hills and villages, to look for riches in the city. Now it sees their children and grandchildren returning, coming not to stay but to relax and to revive their spirits, in search, perhaps, of something which their ancestors took for granted—the timeless certainty of nature. ◐

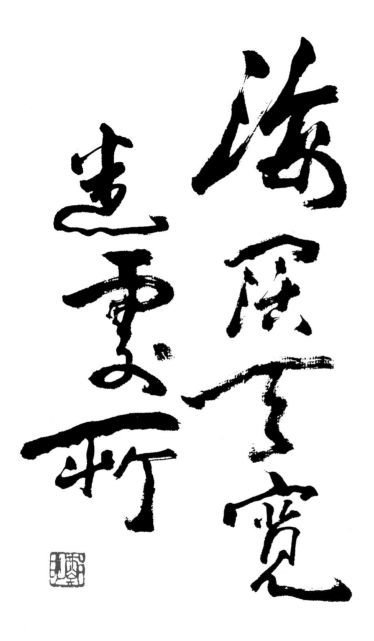

Lost in an expanse of sea and sky.

海 闊 天 寬 迷 處 所

西灣
Sai Wan

Ham Tin

Tolo Channel

Ngau Yee Shek Shan

Ngam Tau Shan

Kai Kung Shan

Pak Tam Au

Lui Ta Shek

Kei Ling Ha

from Pak Tam Au
to Kei Ling Ha
10.2km
北潭凹至企嶺下

Stage Three starts with a steep climb, first up stone steps and then over the grassy upper slopes of Ngau Yee Shek Shan, or Cow's Ear Mountain.

Away to the northeast lies the western arm of Long Harbour. A ferry heading back to Wong Shek Pier barely ripples the water, and a bright flotilla of windsurfers looks like a shower of tiny fireflies, dancing on the sea. In the distance is the island of Tap Mun, emerald in a sea of turquoise.

To the southwest, the view stretches for miles, across Sai Kung and Port Shelter, and on through a break in the hills at Silverstrand to Chai Wan at the eastern tip of Hong Kong Island, those distant towers a reminder that the city is, after all, not far away.

Most dramatic and unexpected is the view ahead, across glorious hills and plunging valleys, spread round in a huge natural bowl. The eye scans the horizon and finds no sign of human life. In this most crowded of cities, here is space.

There is, in fact, just one settlement in these deserted hills—Cheung Sheung, tucked away be-hind trees and a favourite site for weekend camp-ers, who lug enormous quantities of supplies up the hill to barbecue—whole chickens, sacks of char-coal, even a cardboard tray filled with eggs. The sizzle of sausages is drowned by laughter and pop music, but while the hikers relax the dogs of Cheung Sheung are on the prowl, skulking around the bar-becue area, a few paces back from the fire, awaiting their moment to snap up a discarded bone.

On weekdays, when the hikers are away in their offices, factories and schools, Cheung Sheung is once again a remote hilltop hamlet, unserved by roads, untouched by sophisticated city life. In Vic-toria Park on New Year's Eve, city folk pay thou-sands of dollars for a choice spray of cherry blossom, to be taken home and placed beside the laser disc player, secured by pretty red ribbons. A Cheung Sheung farmer simply walks out into the hills and breaks off a large branch of Chinese New Year flower, the shrub whose pretty pink bells decorate the hillsides at this time every year. He takes his branch home and plonks it in an old wine jar. There it stands, outside his hut, unpretentious, covered in blossom and a celebration all of its own.

The Trail sweeps on around the hills, leading the walker down, up and then down again, to the foot of Kai Kung Shan and the start of a long, rough climb.

Exhausted, the walker sits on a rock at the summit and watches a hawk circling. Suddenly the bird freezes, hanging almost motionless in the sky and ready to fall like a stone on unsuspecting prey. Two minutes and more it waits, holding steady in the breeze, eyes piercing the undergrowth for signs of life. Then, finding nothing, the bird veers away and drifts gracefully on towards Ma On Shan, until it is just a speck in the sky. The walker stands up and, legs aching, heads slowly in the same direction.◑

靈山多秀色

The mountains in beauty dressed...

靈 山 多 秀 色

Ngam Tau Shan

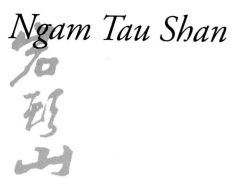

Lui Ta Shek • Kai Kung Shan 雷打石、雞公山

Tolo Channel 赤門海峽

Ma On Shan

Kei Ling Ha

Ngong Ping

Buffalo Hill

Tate's Cairn

*from Kei Ling Ha
to Tate's Cairn
12.7km*
企嶺下至大老山

The path leads up the wooded lower slopes of Ma On Shan, where unseen threads of cobweb brush the walker's face. It is the moment before dawn, when the sun lies hidden behind the hills to the east and the air is still cool and refreshing. Two men, mindful of the impending heat, are already at work, building a chamber to house the remains of their ancestors in large stone jars.

Wong Chuk Yeung village lies almost hidden behind the trees, but the walker catches a glimpse of its cream coloured houses, bathed in soft early sunlight. Away in the distance, fishing boats lie at anchor in Port Shelter and the sepia water is flat calm.

The path leads on up stone steps, through woods which even after a fortnight without rain are cool and damp, and then on up the grassy mountain face. The sun climbs with the walker. Buttercup orchids turn their pretty yellow faces and butterflies settle on rocks and spread their wings, all seeking the morning sun and basking in its warmth.

Thousands of people glimpse Ma On Shan every day, for it towers over Sha Tin, Tai Po and the new town which bears its name. It is soft and green on a summer day, black and stern in storms. Yet its true beauty is seen only here, close to the summit, where the walker lies in the grass on a clear morning and gazes into the very heart of the mountain, awed by its rugged power and permanence.

The Trail turns south towards Pyramid Hill, where a path runs with almost clinical precision straight up the ridge to the summit. The Trail skirts the hill and then crosses Ngong Ping plateau, where melastoma bushes are in a midsummer profusion of blossom and bamboo orchids pout their purple tongues. There are spectacular views of Sai Kung and Sha Tin.

The sun that was still rousing itself when the walker set out is now wide awake and scorching the land. The climb to Buffalo Hill is hard work, but it opens up a new perspective, as Sai Kung and Sha Tin are suddenly shut out and the sweep of hills behind Ho Chung comes into view.

A fine stone path leads down the face of Buffalo Hill and after crossing Heather Pass it is a short climb to the Boy Scouts' Gilwell campsite and the end of the Stage. But there is time for a last look back across the mountains, over Buffalo Hill to Ma On Shan. The sky has clouded over now and the summit looks dark and distant, but the memory of its face remains fresh, one of the Trail's lasting images. 🜚

Rivers and heavens, so vast... endless clouds.

江天空闊雲容漫

馬鞍山

Ma On Shan

Ngong Ping

水牛山

Buffalo Hill

Beacon Hill

Lion Roc

Tai Po Road

Eagle's Nest

Victoria Harbour

Tate's Cairn

*from Tate's Cairn
to Tai Po Road
10.6km*
大老山至大埔道

Hong Kong is commonly portrayed as the ultimate city, a place where people are tucked away in high-rise blocks like papers in a filing cabinet and every square metre of available space is covered in concrete. There are moments along the Trail when such cliches seem absurd—on the windswept coastline of Big Wave Bay, for instance, or up in the swirling clouds of Tai Mo Shan—but Stage Five starts with a rude reminder of urban Hong Kong.

The walker descends from Tate's Ridge to find Kowloon spread out below. Traffic teems along the major roads and the discordant bang of piledrivers and grind of stone crushing equipment float up the hillside. The city is throbbing with energy. Yet at this height and distance it all seems rather artificial, like some huge working model, for the people who power the great city machine are invisible.

The Trail runs down Shatin Pass Road, before shooting straight up Unicorn Ridge, on the way to Lion Rock. Rain clouds roll in from the east, darkening the hills and chilling the air; raindrops spit onto the dusty path and refresh the weary walker. Then the shower passes and there is a wonderful moment of silence, for the path has turned and the city left behind. The way now is along wooded paths around the north face of Lion Rock, and it is easy to leave the Trail and climb to the top of one of Hong Kong's most familiar landmarks. Seen from afar, the summit does indeed resemble a lion, sitting calmly above his city pride, but the perspective is lost at close range and the rounded lines of the lion's body and head are actually comprised of many jagged rocks.

The Trail heads west with another climb to Beacon Hill, and then descends to join a nature trail around the hill known as Eagle's Nest. Trees and rocks are well-marked and the path is meticulously swept, but the walker feels hemmed in by the trees and shrubs and yearns for open country.

In some ways Stage Five is the least attractive and least satisfying of all the stages, but by passing so close to urban Kowloon it does demonstrate the most extraordinary aspect of the MacLehose Trail— that here in this ultimate city there is a 100 kilometre walk across countryside which is still remarkably untouched and unspoiled. ◑

花深迷路晚忘歸

Astray in the hills, well past the homeward hour.

花深迷路晚忘歸

Victoria Harbour
維多利亞港

獅子山

Lion Rock

筆架山

Beacon Hill

Eagle's Nest

尖
山

Shing Mun Reservoir

Smugglers' Ridge

Kowloon

Tai Po Road

Stage 6

*from Tai Po Road
to Shing Mun
4.6km*
大埔道至城門水塘

In the wooded calm of Kowloon Reservoirs, another day is beginning. An old man walks slowly up the hill, carrying a songbird in a cage, with his little grandson running and chirruping beside him. On a grassy verge, a group of men and women are doing their morning exercises, lost in silent concentration. Two housewives bustle past, commiserating loudly about disrespectful youth. At the top of the hill, a woman sits in a pagoda with her knees hunched under her chin, gazing pensively across the reservoir. Pale sunlight begins to filter through the branches.

The Trail turns just below Smugglers' Ridge and winds around the hillside towards Shing Mun Reservoir. It is an easy walk, the shortest of the Trail's ten stages, and it takes the walker back in time.

Here, in December 1941, Japanese and British soldiers fought hand-to-hand for Hong Kong. Shing Mun Reservoir, supplying water to Kowloon and Hong Kong Island, was an important prize in itself, but after three days of fighting the Japanese controlled not only the reservoir but the whole Kowloon Peninsula.

The relics of war remain. The Trail runs past underground tunnels which were built as part of a defensive chain right across Kowloon. The tunnels are still in remarkably good condition, and they still bear the London street names which some colonial official presumably thought would be a jolly good wheeze—Charing Cross and Shaftesbury Avenue, and, hidden away in the undergrowth, Regent Street and a sign to The Strand Palace Hotel.

Yet half a century has passed. Today the tunnels are no more than curiosities, and it is hard to imagine these tranquil wooded hills echoing with mortar fire, hand grenades and the screams of dying men.🔊

A splash of faint red suggesting a touch of rain.

一片暈紅疑着雨

Kowloon Reservoirs

Smugglers' Ridge

好指徑

走私徑 *Smugglers' Ridge*

Lead Mine Pass

Grassy Hill

Needle Hill

Shing Mun Reservoir

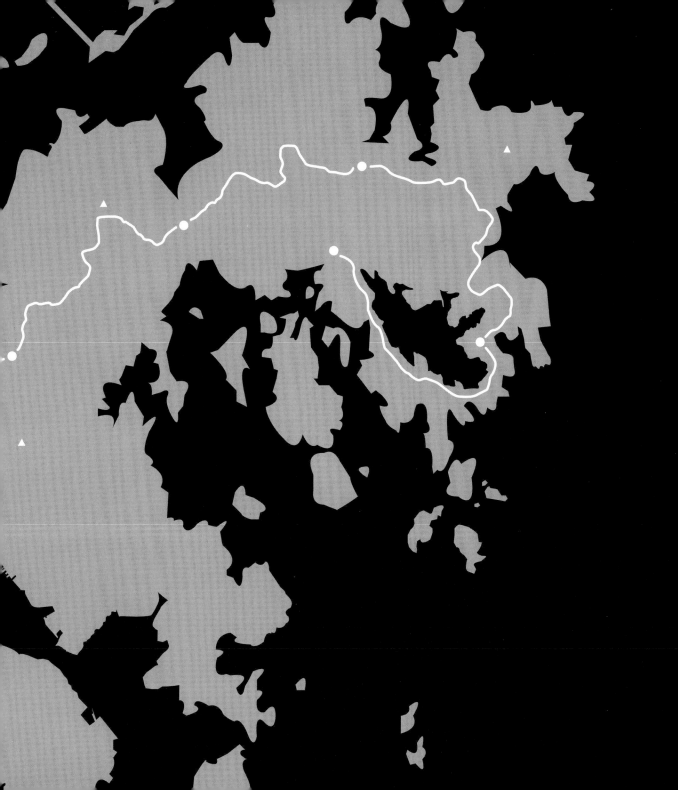

*from Shing Mun
to Lead Mine Pass
6.2km*
城門水塘至鉛鑛凹

The Trail runs up one side of Needle Hill and down the other. Steps lead straight up from the Shing Mun Reservoir's main dam, first through dense green bamboo and then over open ground for the final climb to the summit. Needle Hill is badly eroded and the track offers no shade on hot days, no cover in storms. Only steps, steps and more steps.

The walker arrives, panting but jubilant, at the summit—only to find that a group of students has got there first and the summit is so small that there is hardly room to sit down. Just a few paces ahead, another equally precipitous track leads down the other side.

Walkers with an eye on the clock breathe a sigh of relief when they complete the descent of Needle Hill and set off at a jog towards Grassy Hill, but more leisurely walkers pause at the viewing point. On a clear day, many of the Trail's totems can be seen from here — back to Ma On Shan, Fei Ngo Shan and Lion Rock, and on to Lead Mine Pass and Tai Mo Shan.

A concrete road runs along the ridge of the hills, with the reservoir and its dense woodlands on one side and Sha Tin new town on the other. Beneath the still green waters of the reservoir lie the ruins of Hakka farming villages, which were flooded when the reservoir was built in the 1930s. The villages that dotted the Sha Tin valley survived a little longer, but now they too have disappeared, flooded by concrete.

While Needle Hill is sharp and uncompromising, Grassy Hill is altogether more mellow. Its slopes of coarse upland grass are dotted with boulders, offering a thousand corners of solitude. Sadly, in the dry season these hills are scorched by fires, which also destroy thousands of trees lower down. A hill fire raging out of control is a depressing sight, but nature's regenerative powers are extraordinary. Within a couple of weeks, shoots of green start to appear beneath the blackened, charred stalks. Grasses sprout first, then ferns, and the first shower of rain produces prodigious growth.

After the early stages of the Trail around Sai Kung, the city is never out of sight for long. This is actually one of the Trail's charms, giving the walker a real sense of crossing Hong Kong and offering a new perspective on the geography of Kowloon.

Needle Hill has taken the walker from Kwai Chung to Sha Tin, and now Grassy Hill reveals Tai Po, with its elevated roads winding through the town like a dragon.

A steep path leads down to Lead Mine Pass, named after a mine which stopped production more than a century ago. This was the halfway point on the old path from Tai Po in the north to Tsuen Wan in the south, in the days when the only way of getting from one place to another was by walking. Today, there are highways and tunnels and trains, and north-south traffic through Lead Mine Pass has virtually stopped. Yet it is still a beautiful spot, surrounded by trees and immaculately kept, and a welcome resting place for walkers of the east-west Trail, from Grassy Hill to Tai Mo Shan. ❂

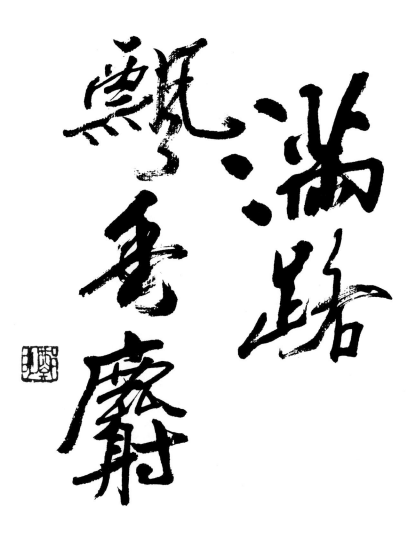

Whiffs of musk scent drifting across the road.

滿路飄香麝

Shing Mun Reservoir

城門水塘

針山

Needle Hill

草山 *Grassy Hill*

Route Twisk

Tai Mo Shan

Lead Mine Pass

from Lead Mine Pass
to Route Twisk
9.7km
鉛礦凹至荃錦公路

Stage Eight is dominated by Tai Mo Shan, Hong Kong's tallest peak.

The climb from Lead Mine Pass is steep and rocky, but it leads to a wonderful ridge path across beautiful high grasslands. This is one of the finest stretches of the whole Trail. In fine weather, it is an exhilarating walk on the top of the world. On darker days, there is mystery and drama, as the wind howls and strangely shaped boulders loom through the mist.

In earlier times, Tai Mo Shan was a working mountain. One of the principal crops was tea, and the Trail passes the stone walled terraces of an old plantation. Today, the tea farmers have been replaced by wireless engineers, who live behind tall fences in a secretive installation at the summit. Unfortunately, the fences also hide the actual summit of Tai Mo Shan, and the walker wanting to stand at Hong Kong's highest point will be disappointed.

Only a handful of hikers approach the summit from Lead Mine Pass, but crowds of people head up from the other side. Large car parks and official viewing points make life easy. In winter they come searching for a trace of frost, and in summer to admire the magnificent views. Charming Kwun Yam Shan is in the foreground, like a scene from a Chinese painting, and away to the west the Shek Kong valley stretches down to Yuen Long.

It has to be said, though, that these views are very often completely hidden. Tai Mo Shan's official name 大帽山 means Big Hat Mountain, but it is known locally as 大霧山, which sounds similar but means Big Fog Mountain. It has the highest rainfall in Hong Kong, and spends much of the year shrouded in mist and low cloud.

When the clouds are really low, visibility is reduced to a few feet and it can be very cold. The birds are silent and the walker feels completely alone. Sometimes, though, the fog is not so dense, and then the walker can stand on the track and watch clouds swirling around in the valleys before rushing up the hillside with a blast of wind. It is a marvellous feeling, like being rolled over by a giant wave.

A snaking road leads down from the summit, and the fields and farms of Chuen Lung come into view. A community was established here more than five hundred years ago, and this is the largest remaining settlement on Tai Mo Shan. An excellent visitors' centre at the end of the road offers much more historical background.◑

會當凌絕頂
一覽眾山小

It's fitting I should assault the topmost peak,
And look down upon the dwarfed mountains.

會當凌絕頂，一覽眾山小

Tai Mo Shan 大帽山

Tai Mo Shan 大帽山

大帽山 *Tai Mo Shan*

Ho Pui Reservoir

Route Twisk

Ngau Liu

Tin Fu Tsai

*from Route Twisk
to Tin Fu Tsai
6.3km*
荃錦公路至田夫仔

At the Route TWISK country parks management centre there is a small brass plaque which reads: "This cairn commemorates the opening of the MacLehose Trail by Sir Murray MacLehose GBE KCMG KCVO on 26th October 1979." Colonial governors often had streets, colleges or hospitals named after them but few memorials have given so much pleasure to so many people as the MacLehose Trail.

Stage Nine is one of the shortest and easiest sections of the Trail. It runs first through a small wood, which is beautifully maintained with all the trees clearly identified. Streams trickle on either side of the track, and a large gold-painted grave is set into the hillside, silent spirits watching the walker pass.

The Trail runs along the ridge of hills that separates Tsuen Wan from the Yuen Long—Shek Kong valley. A lone black bull stands beside the track, dozing in the afternoon sunshine, chewing the cud and flicking his tail lazily at the swarm of flies festering on his flanks. The air cracks with shots from the gun club down the hillside, but the old bull ignores them. This is his country.

Views are glimpsed between the trees. To the south, Tsuen Wan, with its jumble of factories and housing estates, the sprawling container terminals at Kwai Chung and, in the distance, the northern coastline of Hong Kong Island. To the north, a deceptively pretty view of the Shek Kong valley, with Yuen Long and Deep Bay beyond. Shek Kong airfield, once buzzing with British military helicopters, is silent now, save for a solitary small plane which circles the valley like a white butterfly against the green hills.

The track leaves the ridge and meanders down through the woods to Tin Fu Tsai and the head of Tai Lam Chung Reservoir. The walker pauses often —to examine a snakeskin, to peel a soft strip from the paper bark tree, to listen to birdsong or watch a procession of ants. This more intimate look at woodland life is a pleasant contrast to the wild high places that the Trail has crossed, but the sylvan beauty is scarred. Huge pylons strut over the hills, delivering new energy to distant factories and homes. The cables pass over the small farming community of Tin Fu Tsai, which is almost hidden behind trees and bamboos. Fields are overgrown and a few goats and cattle are the only signs of life. In Tin Fu Tsai, as in so many of Hong Kong's traditional farming villages, there seems to be little energy left. ◑

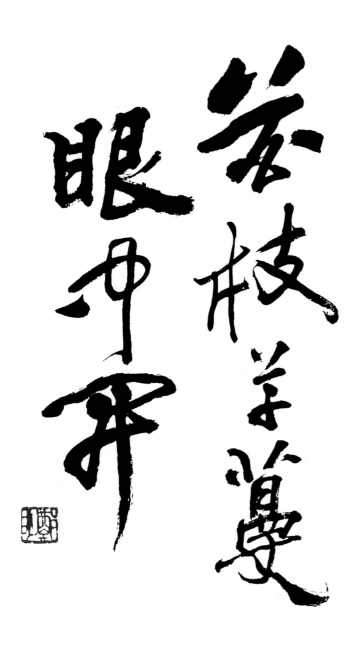

Flowered branches and spreading grass open up in front of one's eyes.

花枝草蔓眼中開

Ngau Liu 牛寮

Ngau Liu

河背水塘 *Ho Pui Reservoir*

Tuen Mun

So Kwun Wat

Tin Fu Tsai

Tai Lam Chung
Reservoir

N

0 0.5 1 2 3km

Stage 10

*from Tin Fu Tsai
to Tuen Mun
15.6km*
田夫仔至屯門

The Trail which started beside High Island Reservoir in the east now draws to a close beside Tai Lam Chung Reservoir in the west, which is fed by an underground tunnel from China and a broad nullah that flows along the lower slopes of Tai Mo Shan. The new water bubbles and tumbles into the reservoir in high spirits after its long journey, but is soon submerged in deep green tranquility.

There is a track to the south which, being higher, offers a wonderful view across the reservoir. It is particularly spectacular as the sun sets behind Castle Peak and burns a golden path across the water. Unfortunately, the Trail takes the northern shore, faithfully winding around every inlet and beside every tributary stream, so that the walker sees only the detail, never the splendid whole.

The Trail runs initially through a dark bamboo tunnel, but then breaks cover to run over sandy ground, where the vegetation is scrubby, with ferns, rose myrtle and small pines. Water flows lazily around low lying, grassy islands, and in one secluded backwater a man sits fishing, a wide-brimmed straw hat protecting him from the sun.

Eventually, the Trail turns away from the reservoir and climbs to a water catchment track that runs flat to the finish. Years ago this track gave a charming view of the So Kwun Wat valley, the sea and the dark hills of Lantau, but now the view is scarred by oil drums, containers, a six-lane highway, a shopping mall and pink tower blocks.

The So Kwun Wat valley has been ransacked by the container companies—or, rather, by short-sighted planners who failed to provide enough storage space in Kwai Chung. Where vegetables were grown for so long, containers are now stacked seven high, rental charges being far more than a year's *pak choi* profits. The little village school, once so smart, is derelict, hemmed in by lorries and weeds.

In the distance, planes make their final descent into the new airport at Chek Lap Kok while others depart for Shanghai, Sydney and San Francisco, the rumble of their engines drowning even the roar of traffic on the highway. Beside the airport, the new town of Tung Chung looks strangely isolated, just a few towers in a fold of the Lantau hills, but who knows what it will look like in fifty years' time. After all, Tuen Mun was once a small fishing port.

After crossing the spectacular unspoilt hinterland of Hong Kong, it is dispiriting to finish the Trail by walking into the unlovely town which is Tuen Mun today. And so as the feet trudge forward, the mind drifts backwards...

...back up into the magical, swirling mists of Tai Mo Shan and the challenge of Needle Hill. Before that, a million lights of urban Kowloon and then the eerie stillness of Shing Mun. Earlier still, the magnificent sweep of beaches around Big Wave Bay and the long climb up Ma On Shan, with hawks circling overhead. And, first of all, the pale morning light and the dawn chorus at Pak Tam Chung, where the adventure started, 100 kilometres ago.

One person has stayed with the walker for every step of the Trail, showing the way and reviving flagging spirits—the little Trailman, painted in black on countless guideposts, a lone figure trudging stoically on, pack on back, always climbing. He is down there now at Pak Tam Chung, waiting for his next companion. ◐

A fresh breeze ripples the waters.

晴風蕩漾落花飛

Tai Lam Chung 大欖涌

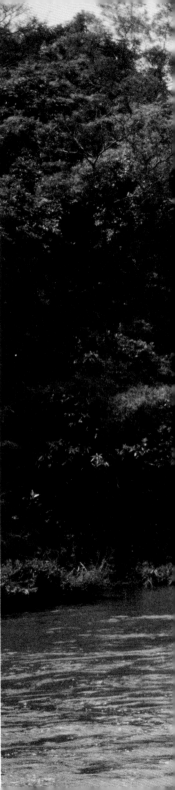

Tai Lam Chung Reservoir

Trailwalker

Once a year the tranquility of the Trail is shattered as people run, walk and will themselves to complete the full 100 kilometres within 48 hours. They are Trailwalkers, taking part in an extraordinary event which has become one of Hong Kong's most popular sporting challenges and raises millions of dollars for charity.

Trailwalker started in 1982 as a military exercise run by the Gurkhas and was opened to the public four years later. Today more than 750 teams of four take part in the event, with organisers tracking 3,000 contestants across some of Hong Kong's most rugged and spectacular countryside.

The start at Pak Tam Chung has the air of a carnival, with contestants in brightly coloured shirts and shorts all talking bullishly of how fit they're feeling and how quickly they're planning to complete the challenge. Most start on Friday morning and aim to run or walk through the night, reaching Tuen Mun on Saturday evening—thirty hours with no sleep and plenty of pain.

Along the way they are met by volunteers and supporters dispensing hot soup, bandages and encouragement at nine checkpoints. At Lead Mine Pass, the leading team runs through on Friday evening, chasing a new record and barely pausing for a swig of water. Most teams arrive some time on Saturday, sitting down on the grass to eat, change

socks and massage tired joints. Then in the early hours of Sunday morning the last of the stragglers loom out of the darkness, having dragged their weary bodies over Needle Hill and Grassy Hill and now facing the last haul up Tai Mo Shan.

If the start resembles a carnival, the finish near Tuen Mun looks like a field hospital. Bodies lie slumped in chairs or sprawled across the floor of a large shed, some swathed in blankets, others groaning quietly. Fatigue has swamped the walkers' minds and their legs have set rigid. An anxious wife cradles a horribly blistered foot, while her husband vows, 'Never again.' They all say that, every year, but most of them return. Indeed, Trailwalker has become a victim of its own success and is now so popular that all available places are filled within fifteen minutes of registration opening. Concerns about safety restrict the number of participants, and every year hundreds of hopeful hikers have to be turned away.

Those who do take part are sponsored for charity, and Trailwalker has become one of Hong Kong's most successful charitable events, raising more than HK$78 million. Oxfam Hong Kong took over from the Gurkhas in organising Trailwalker and uses the money to help poor communities overseas and disadvantaged people in Hong Kong, particularly people with disabilities. In the past, one

third of the money went to the Gurkha Welfare Fund and millions of dollars flowed from the hills of Hong Kong to the mountains of Nepal to create an extraordinary legacy—hundreds of schools, built or equipped with Trailwalker money.

Until their departure from Hong Kong in 1997, the Gurkhas not only organised Trailwalker but also won it. Young soldiers, their limbs and lungs strengthened during childhood in the mountains of Nepal, used to sprint off and run virtually all the way to the finish. The record, set in 1993, is a staggering 13 hours 18 minutes.

For a few participants, that record time is the spur, the dream that drives weary legs and sore feet to run faster through a cold night. Others want to beat the time they set last year, but most are content simply to reach the finish in one piece and to treasure the experience of being in a team of friends and conquering a challenge together.

Old or young, fast or slow, Trailwalkers know that they are part of a unique event along one of the world's most varied and beautiful trails.🌀

The Team

Photography : Tim Nutt, Simone Nutt
Text   : Chris Bale
Painting   : Tao Ho
Calligraphy : Cheng Ming
Design   : Tao Ho
Promotion : Valeria Nutt
Production : The Chinese University Press